I AM D-1

HOW TO CONQUER THE WORLD OF TRAVEL BASKETBALL

I AM D-1

HOW TO CONQUER THE WORLD OF TRAVEL BASKETBALL

*Chris Meadows, M.Ed.
with Jeffrey Shears, Ph.D.*

I AM D-1: How to Conquer the World of Travel Basketball
First Edition Trade Book, 2021
Copyright © 2021 by Chris Meadows, Sr.

To order additional books:
www.IAmD1thebook.com
www.amazon.com

Visit Our Website:
www.IAmD1thebook.com

ISBN: 978-1-952943-07-2
E-book also available

Editorial: Inspira Literary Solutions, Gig Harbor, WA
Book Design: Chad Hamed Design
Printed in the USA

This book is dedicated to my father,
Willie Meadows, Jr.,

Your example, optimism, and
encouragement will always inspire me.

You never gave up.
Can't wait to see you again.

I love you and I miss you.

ROSTER

ACKNOWLEDGMENTS

I believe that it does "take a village," and my life is a reflection of that village. I am thankful and blessed to have always been surrounded by family and friends who have supported and encouraged me to go after my dreams.

First, I want to thank the captain of my family's team, my wife, Glinda. You have been there from the beginning of this D-1 journey. We started down this path together many years ago and you have been there every step along the way. You were there when I scored my first D-1 basket as well my last. You are the arms that keep our family connected. Your support has made the difference. You are my heart and soul and I am so glad we have been able to share this journey together. I love you always and forever. There's no one like you!

And, I thank my son, Christopher Jr.—"C." You are the truth! Your heart has always inspired me to be the best father possible. Your drive and dedication to your craft, along with the love you have for your sister, makes me proud to be your father. Your talent was a major part of this book and project becoming a reality. Thank you, "C"; I love you.

Courtney Monet, you forced me to look deep within myself and grow as a father. Only the two of us will ever know the long hours, days, months, and years that went into developing the tools that made this book possible. You encouraged me throughout this process and your feedback helped make this book better than it would have been. You have always had that "It" factor" and the ability to thrive in the face of adversity. You are a diamond. I love you, Monet.

My mother and father, you always supported me, whatever it was I choose to do. I never heard "NO" from either of you. You always believed I would be successful and gave me love every step of the way.

Thank you to all my siblings: Marilyn, Delores, James, Lawrence, Denise, Deborah, Jeff, and the "twins"—Carla and Karen. When I think of my childhood, you were the best sisters and brothers I could ever have. Your love and support made me into the person I am today. I love you all.

Thank you especially to my brother, Jeff, for the countless days and hours we spent going to gyms and parks to find the best pick-up games in Phoenix. We will forever share the bond and love for the game of basketball. Thank you for always letting me know how much you believed in me. I love you, little bro!

To all the coaches I have ever had the opportunity to learn from, I thank you. Many of the life lessons you instilled in me continue to be a part of my life, and the lessons I have shared with players I have coached and trained.

To the many selfless coaches I have had the opportunity to coach alongside of on the high school and grassroots level: you all have shown me that a coach is truly a servant and I thank you for giving me the opportunity to learn from you all.

Lamont, Charles, Jermaine, Mo, Jeremy, and Shine, thank you all for the countless hours of late nights and early mornings spent talking about the book and helping to strategize on what steps to take next as I pondered the terrain ahead. Thank you.

Angelina, Todd, Greg, Brandon, Mo, Jeremy, Lamont, Charles, Boo, Lewis, and Shandu, thank you for taking time to read the book and share your honest feedback. Forever appreciative.

Jeffrey Shears, thank you for being you. Your steady hand, calm spirit, and ability to communicate open and honestly helped open my thoughts to new perspectives on this journey. This process would have been much more difficult without your support, wisdom, and guidance.

Chad Hamed, you brought the brand to life visually. Your keen sense of direction and knowing exactly what I wanted, even when I was not able to articulate my vision, was amazing. The many days of working into the wee hours of the night paid off. Thank you, my brother.

Willie Campbell, you are the living example of what a true friend should be. You were all in from day one. I do not have words for you. Thank you, my brother. I love you.

To all the parents who have entrusted your sons and daughters to my direction and development: your show of faith in my ability and character will always be appreciated. Thank you!

To every player I have coached or trained: you are the reason why I do it. I thank each one of you for the privilege to work with you and pour into your life through the game of basketball. I have learned more from all of you than you will ever know.

Arlyn, I never knew how much it took to execute at the highest level. Thank you for being humble, patient, and professional while guiding me through the process of editing and making this book a work I will forever be proud of. You are the best!!!!!

Now to Him who has done exceedingly abundantly more than I could ever ask, I thank you for your Grace and Mercy, Lord! Greater love has no one than this, than to lay down his life for his friends and You have shown me what true love is by giving the gift of Your son, Jesus Christ for me. I was able to write this book because of YOU. I can knowingly say, " I can do all things through Christ Who strengthens me."

INTRODUCTION

In my decades of training and coaching basketball and seeing athletes go on to Division 1 programs, I've seen some tremendous success stories, as well as players and families who struggled along the way, for various reasons. Over the years, I have compiled my experiences and observations into concrete thoughts that became the foundation for this book. Here, I attempt to point out some of the roadblocks, challenges, and opportunities that await student athletes and families who pursue D-1 scholarships on the road of travel basketball

This book is written for you, the parent who wants to support and advocate for your child, to prepare and equip you for success. This book is also written for you, the student athlete, as you learn to OWN the journey, and take responsibility for all YOU can do to claim the prize you seek: a scholarship and a place on a D-1 roster. I have endeavored to speak to both audiences in this book—the parent and the player.

The path of D-1 sports is not an easy one, but it IS a memorable one. I hope this book will provide you with the information and direction you need to be successful, and to enjoy every minute of your journey on the road of travel basketball.

~Coach Chris

PRE-GAME NOTE

Speaking from personal experience, I know basketball families are extremely busy and juggle many responsibilities. For that reason, this book was not meant to be a lengthy novel or textbook. Instead, I have composed a book filled with quick-hitters that address critical areas which impact everyone's journey on the road of travel basketball.

I AM D-1 is meant to be an easy read, whether sitting at a long practice, between games at a tournament, or up late at night. Players are also short on time, so this empowering book can be read without feeling like a school assignment.

The purpose is to add valuable nuggets each family and player can use to not only survive but thrive while on this journey of travel basketball.

God bless,

Coach Chris
P.S. Live in the moment . . . because it goes by fast!

PART 1: PURPOSE

#1

SCHOLARSHIPS, NOT TROPHIES

LONG-TERM GOALS

SCHOLARSHIPS, NOT TROPHIES
LONG-TERM GOALS

Years ago, I relocated to Charlotte, North Carolina, in the beginning of the summer—high time for basketball. If you have never lived in a basketball hotbed like the Tar Heel state of North Carolina, believe me when I say you need to witness first hand the parental commitment and intense devotion to training to understand. It was basketball all day, every day, and there were plenty of players who could hoop!

Basketball was more than just a game—it was a lifestyle; the grind was real. I was in basketball heaven and it did not take long for me to get acclimated and entrenched within the local basketball community and jump into the travel basketball machine.

My first experience was on the boys' side and it was serious. My initial meeting with a program director was at

Waddle High School, a nationally elite-level travel program at the time. I walked into the gym and the intensity level, on a scale of one to ten, was a twelve. It was a full-program workout, so there were seventh through eleventh-grade players in the gym. Many of the top players in the city and state were all there, training in this workout. The bleachers were filled with parents, and most of the fathers stood on the baseline, watching intensely. This was not a place for any young player who lacked confidence. It was evident that everyone there knew they were in an environment that produced refined products, appealing to college coaches. Excellence wasn't something to be strived for; it was demanded.

As I grew more familiar with the basketball community, I began to work more closely with players and programs, and eventually I started coaching. I worked heavily with players and families to develop long-term plans to help kids develop and refine their game. Many of the players and families I worked with were a part of that initial program meeting I attended. I would eventually begin to coach a high school varsity basketball team, as well. By this time, I was completely immersed in the local basketball culture and was training players throughout the Metro Charlotte area. This allowed me to establish relationships with many parents and players throughout the state.

The following year, I started coaching a younger travel team for a newly formed organization, and we rapidly gained recognition as one of the top programs for college development not only in the state, but nationally as well. In the first year of the program, I coached a seventh-grade team that was packed with talented players. I made it a point to get to know all the parents personally, and one of the most important questions I would ask the parents and players was, *"What is your long-term goal?"* This was important to me because I was always determined to get the most out of every player, and the ultimate goal for me as a coach was to help each player earn a college scholarship. This question was also important because I didn't want kids who were not "all in." And, to be perfectly honest, I only wanted kids who internally wanted to play at the highest level. This allowed me to know if they were going to be committed and have the personal level of dedication I knew it would take to achieve next-level success.

I quickly realized that some of the kids I coached were still undecided if they wanted to play at the D-1 level, but the irony was that they competed as hard as everyone else. They were not as confident in themselves as the other players were, but I saw they had the potential to make it at the D-1 level, even if they didn't see it in themselves. It became my job to help them realize the potential they had to excel as players who would eventually earn a Division 1 scholarship.

Something I realized early on, as I spoke with parents and players, was that they all had similar goals, but many of them did not know the first thing about how to make their dreams a reality. I felt as if I was watching someone who wanted to go to the beach for a vacation, but who did not have a precise map on how to get there.

Looking Ahead

Each player I spoke with wanted to play Division 1 basketball, and parents were doing everything they could to get their kids on the top teams within the city, regardless of whether or not that program afforded their child the opportunity to grow and develop as a player. Because of this, a good number of these kids did not receive the necessary opportunities to compete and gain the experience of playing in games, which would have allowed them to measure their progress as players. What I noticed was that not many parents placed a high value on developing their kid for long-term success; it was difficult for many to see past the present moment. Many parents were focused on who the top-rated players were at the time or what team won the state AAU title—things that had nothing to do with preparing their child for long-term success.

It seemed to me that every parent wanted to help his or her kid achieve a Division 1 scholarship, but the steps they were taking did not align with their goals. For example, many parents were emphatic about having their kids play on the teams with the best players, as early as fifth or sixth grade.

They would compare their kids to other players of the same age without realizing all players develop and mature at different times/points. There wasn't an emphasis on individualizing the skill development needed to fill in gaps to make every player complete. Bottom line: the overall vision to look beyond the present was not always a priority.

With that in mind, here are a few points to consider:

- Does playing on the top team in your area at an early age really help your child if there is minimal development (i.e., game experience) taking place?

- Is playing on a team that does not have many good players at an early age important?

- Is there a point when a player should move to a more competitive team or program if they are not playing with a competitive team?

These are the questions every family should revisit each year of travel basketball, and the answers will vary for every family. However, there are a few key areas that should be addressed when making these decisions:

1. Is the current environment increasing my child's competitive nature as a basketball player and athlete?

This is extremely important, and I list this at the top because, as we see with professional athletes, players continue to add skill to their games every new season, even at the highest level. This illustrates that developing skills will always be an ongoing process as long as you play the game. However, if you are superiorly skilled yet soft as a player, your skill set will never prevail in an upper-level competitive environment. Being challenged, playing hard, and competing at the highest level are prerequisites for anyone planning to play ball at the Division 1 level. These traits are intangibles, best acquired by immersing players into a competitive environment daily. Many college coaches now have these listed as skills they evaluate, right at the top of their recruiting bullet points. This does not mean that your program or team must be the team that has the best players at ten or eleven years old. You simply want to do your best to be in an environment that is challenging and competitive, and where the coaching and structure are planned with this in mind.

1st Component of D-1 Mindset
COMPETE

2. Does your current basketball environment incorporate real-time skill development with young players during workouts and practices?

When I say "real-time" skill development, I mean skills that are being taught from a fundamental perspective, especially in the early stages of basketball, which are immediately applicable in a game environment. For example, if a player is in sixth grade and is playing travel basketball, he or she should be able to:

- Jab step with either foot off catching a pass
- Pass the ball with either hand accurately off the dribble
- Finish at the rim off a full-speed transition play with either hand
- Change directions with different crossover moves effectively
- Be familiar with the concepts of team defense/shell drill

Some parents work on these skills with their kids away from practice. Building these skills at a young age is extremely important because, as with anything based on sustained growth and development over time, laying a solid foundation at the start will allow that structure to forever stand, regardless of the challenges and adversity it faces along the journey.

As players begin to compete in the arena of travel basketball at the high school level, the order of importance begins to shift, and it becomes exclusively about obtaining a scholarship. With this at the forefront of every player and parent's mindset, the mission takes a turn toward the ultimate goal. When players are in elementary and middle school, it is important to find programs that will foster an environment of competitiveness and real-time skill development. This will help build the foundation needed to excel at that phase of development.

Once players reach high school, however, the focus shifts to being on a team or in a program that has credibility and nationally recognized program directors or coaches who have established relationships with college coaches. If you want to know why this is important at the high school travel basketball level, just go into any showcase event and you will see college coaches migrate to specific courts without knowing any of the players. They will be drawn to specific courts because they know that program's reputation and history for producing players who excel at the college level. Many college coaches will also have history with a particular program's director or coach. Association with a reputable development program is meaningful because it says several things to a college coaching staff about players, such as:

- Players will arrive to campus prepared
- Players will arrive in shape and understand how to get through college practices
- Players will be accustomed to COMPETING at the college level
- Players will be familiar with the intricacies of a college program, including the importance of responsibility and accountability both socially and academically

"Playing for a credible travel program often helps the player in areas that cannot be measured by minutes."

It is always good to win trophies and championships, especially when it is the result of hard work and dedication; however, winning trophies at the expense of building the proper foundation at an early age can be costly in the end. The ultimate goal is to obtain **SCHOLARSHIPS, not TROPHIES.**

#2

SACRIFICE

ALL IN

SACRIFICE
ALL IN

sacrifice | verb
sac•ri•fice :
to suffer loss of, give up, renounce or destroy especially for an ideal, belief or end

It was mid-December, minutes before 9:00 p.m. on a Thursday night. I had just finished rebounding for my daughter after our high school practice. As I sat in the bleachers waiting for her to get her things, the best player on the boys' varsity team walked into the gym by himself and began to stretch near the back wall. He was only a freshman, and the number one-ranked player in the country in his class.

As he began to stretch, I asked my daughter to start doing her homework, because I wanted to stay for a bit and watch him work out. I was curious to see how hard he was going to go the night before a game, as well as what he was going to work on during his workout.

As I watched him finish stretching, he put on a pair of weighted gloves and began to do ball-handling drills. As he finished up, his trainer arrived and the real training session began. I sat and watched intently as, for the next forty-five minutes, he engaged in what turned out to be a full-court workout.

At times, the workout was physically taxing and forced him to take breaks to catch his breath. This workout was impressive for several reasons, but the aspect that stood out most was his positive attitude. He came in focused and immediately got into his routine. He did not have a parent with him and he did not take out his cell phone. It was late on a school night and he had already practiced for two hours earlier that day. He didn't finish his workout until after 10:00 p.m.

The Deposit

Late-night workouts like this are typical for middle and high school players who are seeking to earn a D-1 scholarship. Practices late into the night and early morning workouts are common for players and families on the road of travel basketball. All the sacrifices made by players on this journey can be categorized as "deposits." Like making a cash deposit into a bank, players who make sacrificial "deposits" into their games will be able to make withdrawals consistently when needed. Any commitment and sacrifice a player makes, regardless of the time of day, allows them to "deposit" into their pursuit of becoming a D-1 player. Over time, these "deposits" are the difference between those who say they want it and those who show they want it.

"Daily deposits are a necessity if you will one day be in a position to sign a National Letter of Intent or cash your check."

2nd Component of D-1 Mindset
CONSISTENCY

Many young people who strive to play at the D-1 level have such a passion to grab their dream that most people outside of their inner circle cannot comprehend or relate to such a commitment. We often hear comments such as, "That kid doesn't have a life," or, "I can't believe their parents are forcing them to do that," and the most common comment, "They don't get to be a kid like everyone else." I heard this about my own kids, and I have heard it about almost every young person I know who has grown up with a pursuit to play at the Division 1 level. There is nothing normal about the level of commitment required to build the skill and intangibles required to become a Division 1 athlete. **There is also nothing normal about receiving a full scholarship to pay for your undergraduate degree as well as the additional benefits and perks that accompany this reward (a Division 1 scholarship).** The sacrifice required can only be summed up with the old adage, "It's a labor of love!"

I am familiar with many high school basketball players who have missed events that most people see as lifetime milestones, such as high school proms, award ceremonies, and even family weddings. It is true that the pursuit of playing basketball at the D-1 level requires a commitment that will take players away from situations and opportunities in which their friends will participate. These are decisions that each player and family will have to approach individually. Every player has different interests and personalities, and some events are more important than others; it is up to the player and the parents to decide how to prioritize more "normal" activities against the demands of the nonstop travel basketball schedule.

Family Sacrifice

Yes, we are talking about the extreme sacrifice required for basketball players who are pursuing their D-1 reward. This extreme level of SACRIFICE also affects the entire family of those who play travel basketball.

When playing at the elite level, most families know their normal schedule will be interrupted on a daily basis throughout the year. There will be early morning workouts before school as well as late nights when you may not leave the gym till well after midnight. Some players and families may have to drive to different cities or neighboring states for practice on weeknights and/or weekends. Many parents will need to adjust work schedules to accommodate frequent tournaments, practices, and daily workouts.

It is important to understand that if you generally like to take a family vacation in July, it is probably not going to happen if you are playing showcase basketball. Many families will try to squeeze in a vacation in August to avoid the hectic travel basketball demands of July. June is equally hectic with high school ball, team camps, summer leagues, and elite camps. This schedule makes June off limits as well. I have a close friend who has taken the entire month of July off from work for the past seven years because his child has played elite travel basketball since the seventh grade. My friend and his wife understood from the beginning the demands of this schedule, and they made it a point to travel with their child and enjoy the time as a family.

Another area of travel basketball that is rarely discussed but impacts all parties involved is the financial sacrifice. Regardless if you are part of a sponsored travel program or a

SACRIFICE

local travel team, the financial sacrifice required is not always considered during the initial planning phases. Most families I have worked with were primarily concerned with the program fee for the season. Team fees are generally discussed when making inquiries, or in the initial program meetings. These are what I call "window fees" (what you see up front); most teams have them and these fees generally can be paid at one time or broken into installments, depending on the program.

Once most families get past the window fees, there are certain necessities that can't be avoided (even if playing for a sponsored program)—and trust me, they add up! Most events start games on Friday nights, but say you are scheduled to arrive Friday for an early Saturday game. Parents will have lodging accommodations for two nights ($125.00/night average cost). The entry fee for most showcase events for a day pass can add up as well ($20/day per person). Let's not forget that these days can be long, and staying in a hotel means eating out is also a must. Some hotels provide complimentary breakfast, which helps. If you decide to eat at the facility snack bar, a fast-food outlet, or a sit-down restaurant, you will most likely eat twice both days (at least $10.00/meal twice per day, per person). Each player generally has a sports drink for hydration during and between games ($3.00/drink). There are many other costs that are normally part of the weekend but let's remain focused on standard expenses that most families will incur without adding any extra curriculars.

AVERAGE WEEKEND TRAVEL TOURNAMENT
EXPENSES (Family of Three)

- HOTEL, Friday/Saturday: $250.00
- EVENT ENTRY FEE: $120.00
- MEALS/DINING $120.00
- PLAYER SPORTS DRINKS $20.00

Standard Tournament Weekend Expense Budget:*   **$510.00**

(*on the conservative side)

This two-day budget for a family of three will grow exponentially during the month of July when there are two live recruiting periods that extend for six days per live period, equaling almost half of the month. July alone has the potential to cost a family $3,000 to $6,000 by itself.

As you can see, **SACRIFICE** will be required by every family that decides to travel this road. The financial sacrifice should be considered because it extends far beyond the player. So, while the travel basketball experience will surely be filled with memories and shared experiences that will last a lifetime, there is a price both the player and the family have to pay. Sacrifice is not optional; it is a toll you must pay once you get on the road of travel basketball.

#3

PLAYING UP

NOT IF, BUT WHEN

PLAYING UP
NOT IF, BUT WHEN

Allowing a player to "play up" at a young age has always been a major debate. Playing up versus playing with older, bigger, stronger, and faster players at a young age can yield positive benefits. However, it can also have negative consequences if not managed properly.

I have seen it work for some players and I have witnessed it be discouraging for others. There are some players who have played up from their first year of travel basketball and have achieved success. Then there are others, who also have played up since they began playing travel basketball, who have never been better than average, but their parents were content to say that their child was "playing up."

There is another perspective on playing up—a route some players and parents take—which involves a player participating on a team with peers who are in the same grade. That entire team will play up versus older competition and will be able to play together for years to come without splitting up their team. Regardless of which route you decide to take, the decision to play up is one of the most important decisions you will make as a travel basketball family.

First, we can consider that the game of basketball at its purest form is played in the neighborhood, park, YMCA, or rec center. Most basketball players have stories that generally connect back to one or more of these early neighborhood hoop congregations. These early hoop spots always include playing against older siblings, cousins, or friends. These stories are significant because this is where many players develop the mentality that sparks the mental toughness and competitive nature that shape their inner drive. **The opportunity to play with older players often drives you to expand your limitations as well as builds confidence to help you grow as a player.**

3rd Component of D-1 Mindset
CONFIDENCE

Here are two questions to carefully consider as you decide when the time is right for you to make your move to begin playing up:

1. Is the player physically able to compete with older players without being overpowered or injured?

This goes far beyond the size of the player. You have to know the player personally. I have seen many young players who are physically much bigger than their peers. Although a player might have the size to play at an eighth-grade level when they are in fifth grade, developmentally they might not be ready to compete with players who are far more aggressive, and mentally and emotionally more mature. When any player is mentally and emotionally far younger than his or her peers, placing them into a competitive environment could be dangerous. The physical aggression and intensity of older players is often a major factor when deciding if a player is ready to compete against older competition.

I had the unfortunate experience of seeing a team that was both physically and emotionally unprepared to compete against older players. I was at the eighth-grade AAU nationals in Memphis, Tennessee, where I watched one of the most talented teams in the country. They were playing a team that was far less talented and many of the players on the opposing team were younger players. Not only were they outmatched in talent; they did not have the intensity or physical strength to compete on the same level as their opponents. As a result, many of the players on this team were injured and one player's injury resulted in a concussion.

As I watched the game, it was evident that the younger, smaller team was not only undersized and physically underdeveloped, but they also lacked the skill to compete at that level. In this situation, playing up against older competition was more of a health hazard for the younger, smaller, less-skilled team. They were not only outmatched physically, but they were also much younger from a cognitive perspective. When you add up the physical, mental, and emotional gaps between these two teams, there was little the younger team could take away from the experience to help them grow as players.

Another perspective on playing up is the player who has chosen to play within their proper age group/grade. I do not see this as a major issue when the player is younger, especially in elementary and middle school. Playing your grade, or on a team that is your grade, can have long-term benefits while also fostering lifelong relationships with same-age peers. Playing your grade can also be a good way to build confidence for many players who may not be ready to play against older, more talented players on a constant basis. As mentioned earlier, all players mature at a different pace, and there is nothing wrong with a player playing his or her grade while developing physically and building the skill set and confidence needed to move to the next phase of growth. This decision often has great benefits for the future.

There is an unfortunate trend of parents feeling pressured to have their child play up in grade, even if he or she is not ready developmentally as a player. As with constructing anything you want to last, building a solid foundation is most important. Allowing each player the time to mature at his or her own pace is critical for long-term success.

2. Has your child experienced success playing with the same age group before moving them up?

I have watched extremely talented teams who were all in the same grade stick together and, instead of beating the breaks off teams their age, their coaches and parents agreed to play them up as a unit. I had the opportunity to watch one team in particular do this over a period of years.

This group started playing together when they were in sixth grade. Once they started playing up, they took their lumps, and there were many lopsided losses. But, experiencing losses at the hands of older teams was not an issue for the players, coaches, and parents. This team had dominated their own age group and won AAU state championships, so there was nothing more they were going to gain from continuing to win trophies. As the team continued to play, they began to improve. Initially they thought they were an exceptionally talented group as they measured themselves against their true peer group. Once this group began to play against older players, they were humbled and, as a result, the players adjusted their mindset. The team soon realized their potential was far greater than their actual level of performance. These players were capable of playing harder, being more aggressive, and making smarter and faster decisions. Playing up in grade transformed their mental approach to the game and, as a result, they all raised their level of expectations individually and collectively.

By choosing to take their lumps early as a unit and play up as a team, every one of these players ended up signing with successful Division 1 programs as seniors in high school. This group also produced a total of seven McDonald's All-Americans, eight Jordan Brand All-Americans, and two Team USA Players. I honestly believe that the decision to play this group up in grade when they were in middle school transformed them mentally and pushed them to raise their level of play. Initially this group was slightly overconfident after dominating their age group, but after playing up they realized they had many areas to improve. This allowed them to grow as players, as well as opening the eyes of their parents to see the bigger picture of competition and talent on a more comprehensive scale. As a result, they measured themselves against all talent, regardless of age.

"Remember, no player can sign a National Letter of Intent until November of his or her senior year of high school, regardless of how talented they may be."

This is important to remember because many parents make decisions to play a player up in grade when they are simply not ready to embrace a new and more competitive environment. I have witnessed well-intentioned parents make decisions to move their child up when the player had never been dominant or had a moderate level of success at their grade level. Before moving up to compete against older more skilled players, it is imperative for a player to experience in-game success with peers of the same age or grade.

Confidence Is Key

Being confident as a young basketball player comes from achieving success during game situations. When a player begins to play up against older, bigger, stronger, more skilled players before experiencing success against players of the same age or grade, it can inhibit the success needed to build confidence. It can be easy for parents to forget that all players mature differently. I have witnessed some parents make the mistake of trying to keep up with other players' progress by moving their child up when the child was simply not ready to make the jump.

Avoid putting your child under pressure by comparing his or her trajectory of growth and development to that of their peers. Going back to our earlier mention about how each player and family should define their goals, remembering your long-term goals as a family should guide this decision. As a reminder, it's important to put on blinders and disregard what decisions other players are making, and do what is best for you and your family at this moment in time.

Once a player gets to high school, it becomes more about the individual travel program and its philosophy. Many players begin to play 17U once they get to high school. This is understandable for those who are ready because there is no age requirement to compete on the varsity level. There are oftentimes fourteen or fifteen-year-old players on the court competing with eighteen-year-old players in every varsity basketball game. However, if you play for an elite travel program, you may have upper class All-Americans playing on the older teams, and this will often prevent talented young players from playing up in elite travel programs. If this is the case for you, college coaches understand, and will typically scout the younger teams in the elite programs because they realize the depth of the talent pool in these programs.

The opposite is true if you are playing travel basketball for a team that may not be part of an elite travel program. You may have an opportunity to play up on an older team at an earlier age due to the lack of elite players in the program. This scenario happens quite often, and has allowed players who were not as heavily recruited to gain valuable experience as well as time and opportunity to grow. For some players, this has led to exposure and recruiting opportunities that may not have come if they had been playing for organizations with more talented players.

It is important to remember that college coaches will continue evaluating players until the spring of their senior year. Regardless of how talented you are, no player can sign a National Letter of Intent until November of his or her senior year. Some players may receive college scholarship offers very early in the process and others may receive scholarship offers in the spring of their senior year. And, there are some who will not receive a college offer until even later than this. (If this is you, please read the section on recruiting.)

The road of travel basketball is a marathon, and if your long-term goal is to earn a college scholarship, it's imperative to know and understand this process. It is often said, "Trust the process," but it is even more important to know and understand the process. In the end, it doesn't matter how early you arrive at the party, just as long as you get there. As you contemplate the notion of playing up, it is not a matter of "IF" you will PLAY UP, but "WHEN" you should PLAY UP.

#4

BALANCE

PICK-UP VS. TRAINING

BALANCE
PICK-UP VS. TRAINING

"How often should I train versus how often should I play pick-up?" This is a question I am asked frequently. While both playing pick-up ball and training are a necessity, finding the proper balance is critical.

Benefits of Playing Pick-Up

In today's game, the skill level is as high as it has ever been; however, the feel, pace, and instincts that come along with playing pick-up ball are difficult to acquire in training sessions. There are also players who do not train often but play a lot of pick-up ball. Many of these players are aggressive and confident, but lack the pinpoint detail needed to become elite players. **Playing pick-up ball and training are both essential if you want to excel in an organized environment.** Elite players work hard to find that perfect balance.

Many of the players today train on a daily basis and have not had the opportunity to experience the joy and excitement that come from playing pick-up ball. The creativity, spontaneity, and instincts acquired from playing pick-up are often noticeable when watching young players on the court. Those who play pick-up ball often develop a feel and pace for the game that comes from competing without the comforts of structure, clocks, whistles, and adult intervention. These nuances of the game that are developed from playing pick-up ball are invaluable.

Playing pick-up also provides opportunities for players to experiment and apply skills they have worked on with their trainers. When you hear a coach talk about being "savvy," or see a player doing little things that seem natural, they have what is called a "sixth sense"; these qualities are by-products of playing pick-up ball.

When you talk to most professional basketball players about when they first fell in love with the game, almost all of them will go immediately back to a time when they were young, and it usually involved playing basketball in rec leagues, park 3on3 games, or playing pick-up with friends. I listened to a conversation with Michael Jordan where he talked about how he developed his inner competitive nature from 1on1 battles with his brother in the backyard. I interviewed Skylar Diggins, after a Team USA practice, and she told me, "Competing is a way of life, no matter where I play." Where do you think that kind of love for the game was developed?

When I train players in small groups, I break down my sessions into four phases: Teaching Phase, Repetition Phase, Application/Reaction Phase, and Competition Phase. The Competition Phase is always the phase players enjoy the most, where they actually compete. Many players do not always have a chance to put their skill development to the test and flat-out compete. There are simply times when players need to go up and down to keep their timing and instincts in rhythm—and there is no better avenue to acquire that feel than playing pick-up ball.

As important as it is to play pick-up ball, especially for younger players into middle and high school, it is equally important to train and develop a strong foundational skill set that will be a necessity at the higher levels of basketball. Training should be an integral part of every player's basketball diet and it should be carefully structured and planned.

As the game has progressed and the stakes have become higher, player development has become an essential part of the game. Many players and their families are on a mission to earn a D-1 scholarship and they understand that training is a key factor in obtaining their goal.

Training

Having a good trainer who is knowledgeable and able to teach can be a difference maker. Today, the game of basketball is immensely predicated on skill. There has been a transition from being overly focused on athleticism and highlight plays to placing more value on players who are able to impact the game with a high level of skill. Players like Steph Curry, Luka Doncic, Elena Della Dunn, and Kelsey Plum can take over a game without ever dunking the basketball; their ability to shoot the ball and maneuver in any situation makes them difficult to defend. When I talk with the best players at every level, they all have one thing in common: they commit to consistent and rigorous training schedules.

"Training should have different purposes based on each player's level of development."

For young players, training should be comprehensive and intentional, to build a broad range of skill. This is important regardless of size or position. Basketball has become a global game and is now a sport that is truly "positionless." This means that if you want to be able to compete and add value, it is simple: you must be able to play as many positions and guard as many positions as possible. **This can be a reality for every player if they have a broad skill set that can be transferred to every spot on the court.** Building this skill set at an early age is a necessity if your desire is to earn a college scholarship. So, training properly at an early age and building a broad skill set should be a priority for younger players.

As players get older and transition into high school,

training should become more purposeful and specific. A player should try to always include shooting when training, and there should be days when he or she shoots exclusively in isolation. When you watch high-level college basketball games, there are two areas that consistently stand out: the high number of three-point shots taken and how deep the players shoot those three-point shots. With such major emphasis on shooting in today's game of basketball, all players should put more time into becoming high-level shooters. This will allow coaches to space the floor and increase a player's chance of grabbing a college coach's attention. This is a major reason why skill development in the high school years must become more focused and intentional. It also emphasizes why skill development must be comprehensive at younger ages, to allow players to focus more on specifics at the high school level.

I once had a high school player and parent contact me after their travel season ended and they were in the process of getting ready to plan to train for the next season. So, I asked them if they had taken the time to review their previous high school season as well as the travel season they had recently completed, to evaluate and assess performance. They had not thought about this before we talked, so I asked the player, "What did you do extremely well during both your high school season and travel season?

The player answered me with, "Coach, my jumper was cookin' during high school season, but it was off with my travel team." After asking more questions, I quickly discovered that during this player's high school season, he had been a primary ball handler and most of his shots had come off the dribble, but during travel ball, he had played with other point guards and did not handle the ball as much. Most of his shots came off screens or were catch and shoot. It was apparent that this player was skilled at shooting off the dribble but needed to work on becoming a better shooter off the catch and coming off screens. A post-season assessment like this can assist you with being more specific with your training to help you continue to improve your game.

HIGH SCHOOL BASKETBALL
PLAYER 12-MONTH CALENDAR

AUG • SEPT • OCT
HIGH SCHOOL PRE-SEASON
- DEVELOP/IMPLEMENT TRAINING SCHEDULE
- STRENGTH & CARDIO PLAN
- BE SPECIFIC: DAYS OF WEEK/DURATION
- TARGET IMPROVEMENTS & DOCUMENT GAINS

NOV • DEC • JAN • FEB
HIGH SCHOOL SEASON
- DAILY PRACTICES/ GAMES
- DEVELOP PRE/POST PRACTICE: 15-MIN. WORKOUT
- BALANCE ACADEMICS W/ PRACTICES: TIME MANAGEMENT
- ADEQUATE REST & DIET

MAR • APR • MAY • JULY
TRAVEL BASKETBALL PREP & PLAY
- REVIEW HIGH SCHOOL SEASON
- REFORMULATE MENTALITY TO TRAVEL BASKETBALL
- CONSTRUCT NEW PLAYER DEVELOPMENT SCHEDULE
- ASSESS & REVIEW RECRUITING W/ COACH & PARENTS

JUNE
HIGH SCHOOL TEAM MONTH
- HIGH SCHOOL TEAM SUMMER LEAGUE
- TEAM CAMPS
- TARGET ELITE CAMPS (BE INTENTIONAL)
- PREPARE MIND & BODY FOR LONG MONTH OF JULY

Training Frequency

The frequency of training should be based on a variety of factors. First, training frequency has to be in conjunction with the time of year as well as the player's stage of development. Let's focus on the training frequency for high school players.

If you are a high school basketball player, you have specific commitments based on the yearly high school basketball calendar. The availability to train as well as the type of training high school players engage in will be determined by the time of year (see illustration above).

One important aspect of player development for high school players is to mix it up between individual and small group training sessions. Individual training sessions can allow you to be specific with target areas for the individual player. If you have a specific skill set you are working to improve or correct, individual training sessions can be the answer you need to accomplish your goal quickly.

Small group training sessions also provide important benefits that can catapult player performance, especially if players play similar positions, and are in an environment where players feed off one another. These sessions create an atmosphere that breeds competition and often forces players to develop and display a deeper level of concentration than they would experience during individual sessions. As they say, iron sharpens iron.

A Note about Female Players and Playing Pick-up

It is generally easy to identify the girls who play pick-up ball: their game jumps out as more natural and it flows. Unfortunately, playing pick-up is an area in which many girls do not participate enough. I encourage all girls to make an effort to find and/or create opportunities to play more pick-up ball.

Pick-up is a key element in helping girls transition their game to becoming natural and free flowing. Playing pick-up will also help girls make the transition from reacting to anticipating when in game situations. It will also help speed up the decision-making process and add confidence to their game. Each of these benefits will help girls play the game with more fluidity and confidence as they grow older. While it may be a challenge to make these pick-up games a reality, the payoff will benefit for a lifetime.

Pick-up Ball in Moderation

I have already listed many of the benefits that playing pick-up ball provides earlier in this chapter. I want to make it clear: playing pick-up is beneficial and should be played. Pick-basketball is the nucleus of the game and out of it flows the joy of the game. However, that being said, especially for high school players, there are times when you should temper playing pick-up ball.

I have always believed that when players start the high school season, they should limit their pick-up ball opportunities, especially the more the season progresses. The closer they get to the state playoffs, the more they should turn to getting up shots outside of practice and working with a trainer to stay sharp individually. Reducing most pick-up ball opportunities can also prevent unnecessary injuries.

I can recall a situation with a rising high school star who was in her junior year. Her team was making a strong push toward the state championship. The night before the state semi-final game, she was playing pick-up ball at the Y and fractured a bone in her foot. She missed the Final Four game as a result of the injury and the team also lost in the state semi-finals. This situation is an example of knowing when to limit playing pick-up ball. The high school season is unforgiving, and it is a brief window of opportunity. Also, most high school teams are more heavily dependent on their best players, unlike travel basketball teams, and an injury during the high school season can potentially have a negative impact and derail the hopes for the entire team.

In today's quest to improve your game, there has to be a healthy mix of training (player development) and pick-up ball. This mix will vary per player but the skill set needed to be effective in a structured environment will require hours of training to hone your game and elevate your performance.

As a player, you never want to lose the instinctive nuances of the game, or the opportunity to incorporate into your game the skills you are working. This is so important that Michael Jordan was the first player to have what is called a "love-of-the-game clause" in his contract. This allowed him the freedom to be able to play basketball, pick-up, or exhibition games whenever and wherever he wanted to play.

So, the goal is to maintain a healthy balance between both training and pick-up ball if you want to continue to evolve your game as an elite basketball player.

I AM D-1

TRAIN VS. PLAY MODEL

PICK-UP VS. TRAINING

This model is a reference if you want a good place to start as you balance your training and playing schedule.

Based on interviews of 100 Division 1 basketball players on their training vs playing schedule when they were in high school.

50%
Player Trainer

25%
1v1, 3v3, 5v5
Open gym

25%
Autonomous
Workout

#5

SELECTING A TRAINER

THE RIGHT FIT

SELECTING A TRAINER
THE RIGHT FIT

"Do I need a trainer?"

Many people don't want to answer this question head on, and some will go as far as to say when they were young they didn't have a trainer and they don't see why players today feel they need one. But, the reality is that, over time, trainers have shifted from a luxury to a near necessity.

Today's game of basketball is played far differently than even ten years ago; players today are shooting the ball much deeper, the spacing on the floor is extended further, and the skill level is visibly more advanced. So, to answer the question, "Do I need a trainer?" the answer is simple. If you want to maximize your talents and expand your game, you will benefit from having a trainer who is proven and understands what you need as a player.

The Importance of a Trainer

When you look at Serena Williams, Tiger Woods, Simone Biles, and Roger Federer—all of whom undoubtedly have transcended their respective sport—what do they all have in common? Regardless of how much success they have achieved, each one of these athletes has an individual coach or trainer. When you study the elite basketball players, all of them have personal trainers who are familiar with the nuances of their games. This is important and necessary in order to help them continue to improve and expand their effectiveness and lengthen their careers.

Now, if the most successful athletes in this generation all have individual trainers to help them improve their performances, then up-and-coming basketball players will be able to drastically benefit from a trainer as well. Here is an example of how detailed and specific training can help immediately.

I had been training a college player who played in one of the toughest conferences in the country and this player's stock was rising nationally. The first few games of the season were solid, and the national media was beginning to talk more and more about this player's professional possibilities as a first-round draft pick. The next two games were average and after talking with him, I could tell his confidence was sliding.

The team was scheduled to play in a Thanksgiving

Tournament that would be nationally televised, and they would be playing the number one team in the country in their first game of the tournament. I had two days of training with the player before the tournament, and I wasn't going to let any time go to waste. I was able to look at video from the previous two games and break it down to create a specific two-day plan to get his confidence back and polish a few trouble areas of his game.

After reviewing the game film, I realized immediately the biggest problem was that he was not taking open shots (sounds simple, I know). He was taking a lot of heavily contested shots and he was also over penetrating. Once we talked about the areas that needed to be addressed, we focused on catching and shooting spot-up open threes without hesitation. We also focused on taking and knocking down the mid-range pull-up instead of crashing into defenders in the lane.

Since this player had the ability to get into the lane easily, we worked on kicking out to shooters once he got in the lane to take advantage of defenders over-helping. This was a simple and narrowly focused two-day plan that included aggressive court work with a lot of what I call "intentional repetition." We had two specific training sessions at 7:00 a.m. both days. Two days later, he was playing against the number one team in the country on ESPN.

"Keep in mind that results from training won't always be measured quantitatively; however, player confidence should invariably be the result of effective training sessions."

The game ended up being close, and the player I had trained was the Player of the Game. Even in a loss, he lifted his team and played an exceptional game while nearly upsetting the top team in the country. He had a stat line of twenty-six points, seven assists, and four rebounds with zero turnovers. I'm not saying the reason for his entire performance was a result of our training sessions, but the things we worked on contributed to his performance and the results were evident. Even in a loss, he was the lead story on ESPN'S Sports Center after the game.

Finding the Right Trainer

Selecting a trainer can be a challenging process. There are basketball trainers everywhere and trying to come up with criteria to select a trainer can be challenging, especially if you are on Twitter, Instagram, or YouTube. If you have found a trainer you feel might be the right fit for you, I would encourage you to go to a training session to get a personal feel and experience the environment before making a decision. Here are four points I encourage you to consider when you are looking for a basketball trainer to help with player development:

1. Knowledge of the game

Today's game is played much differently than in the past. The pace of the game is faster, spacing of the floor is much wider, players shoot the ball much deeper, and the skill set requires every player to be able to handle the ball and shoot it equally as well. We are in an age that plays what is called "positionless basketball." So, finding a trainer who comprehends these concepts ensures they understand the skill set required to be an effective player. I encourage you to watch a full game of basketball at the college level and pay close attention to the following:

- How many three-point shots are taken by players of all positions
- How well every player handles the ball, regardless of size
- How often every player uses fewer than four dribbles to either create a shot or pass to teammates
- How most players are able to defend multiple positions

Understanding these concepts is important because many trainers are focused on teaching players moves that look very impressive, but which are rarely used in a meaningful basketball game at any level. If you are not someone who is knowledgeable about the game, being able to ask a few questions to a potential trainer is important. Questions such as these will be helpful:

- Do you break down videos of players before you start training? (Assessment)
- Do you specialize in one particular area?
- Did you play ball in college or coach? (Knowledge base, not a requirement)
- Do you have any players you have helped develop consistently over time?
- Do you have a methodology for your training? (Similar to my four-phase system I described in Chapter 4)

2. Character

When selecting a trainer, it is imperative to be familiar with the character of the person with whom your son or daughter will be spending time. Depending on the commitment, the player and trainer relationship can sometimes lead to spending double-digit hours per week together. Connecting with someone who can have a positive influence on your son or daughter is extremely important as most player-trainer relationships generally span multiple years.

Another aspect of being an effective trainer is possessing the ability to motivate players internally to master what is being taught, and drive them to want to work with a more renewed sense of purpose when they are by themselves. Finding a trainer who can build trust and is able to become a trusted part of the "family dynamic" is important. If you find an effective trainer, that person will undoubtedly become a part of your extended family. Everyone will share that common thread of interest, which will be seeing and investing in the success of the player, not only on the court but in life, as well. So, finding a trainer you can trust is important because you will eventually develop a relationship that will become more personal and less business the longer the relationship lasts.

3. Effective Communicator and Teacher

Being able to effectively teach as a trainer is a MUST. Many people can and have played the game at a high level, but the art of being able to effectively communicate while breaking down concepts is not as common as you may think. (I have observed this first hand; not only was I fortunate to grow up close to the game from an early age and play it at the Division 1 level, but I also majored in Education in both undergraduate and graduate degrees.)

The ability to effectively communicate and break down information while maintaining an extreme focus on details is a must when looking for a basketball trainer. Being knowledgeable is important, of course; however, being able to effectively communicate what you are teaching is equally important. Over time, you should be able to see pieces of what the player is working on during training sessions applied in game situations. It this is not happening, it may be a good idea to talk with your trainer and tighten up your sessions.

4. Availability/Consistency

Once you have found the trainer you feel is the person to help you improve and take your game to the next level, there is one final area you must discuss before you get started: the availability of a facility. Having consistent access to a gym or facility can at times be a challenge for some trainers, and this lack of availability of a consistent facility could prevent any player from achieving their goals. Many trainers do not own their own facilities and depend on relationships, whether business or personal, to gain consistent gym access.

There are some trainers who are coaches and they may have access to a school facility. There are some who may work for a basketball facility and may have access to that facility. Then, there are some trainers who may rent space or have relationships with local gyms that will provide access to facilities, allowing them to be consistent. Regardless, be sure to talk with your trainer to get a good understanding of their situation to make sure you can be consistent and continue your development as you strive to improve your game.

Own It and Go Get It!

I have provided four key factors to consider in your process of finding a trainer. You can always add additional factors if you feel you need more information to consider in your decision-making process.

I want to communicate one additional point that all players should know and embrace if they are going to maximize their talent. **There is no replacement for taking ownership and responsibility for the growth and development of your game as a basketball player.** There will never be a substitute for good, old-fashioned, consistent hard work! All great players have to put time in by themselves. Whether in the driveway, park, or a gym by yourself, that alone time in the dark is the only way you will shine under the lights.

A trainer can help shape your game, but only you can make your game. Go get it!

#6

TRAVEL TEAM ROULETTTE
PRIORITIZE, PRIORITIZE

TRAVEL TEAM ROULETTE
PRIORITIZE, PRIORITIZE

Travel basketball is a highly competitive environment and it's not restricted to the court. Club directors and coaches are constantly recruiting players, players themselves are recruiting their friends to play together, and parents are networking with other parents to join their programs. Many of these conversations occur at tournaments and some of these agreements actually happen during the games. Unlike high school basketball, there are no rules preventing players from moving from program to program. Due to a lack of restrictions, players can and do move from team to team frequently, and this happens from tournament to tournament. The high frequency of movement is not as common with younger teams but it goes into overdrive once players get into high school.

In Chapter 1, "Scholarships, Not Trophies," we talked about selecting a traveling team; in this section, I am going to focus specifically on players who are already in high school. As mentioned earlier, travel basketball is a transient environment. Player movement from team to team and program to program is common, and there are several reasons for this. I will dissect the causes as well as share options you may consider as you go through this phase of your journey, including:

- Misinformation
- Not the Right Fit
- Dysfunctional Environment

Misinformation

Sadly, one of the most common and damaging reasons for player movement is misinformation. The amount of information coming at players and their families can be overwhelming and difficult to sift through. The majority of this information is inaccurate and can disrupt long-term growth for players and possibly crush many scholarship opportunities.

I have watched parents make decisions to move their kids from teams that were benefiting them in multiple areas. Many of these moves were made because parents were comparing their son or daughter to other players on the team. This is why it is important—and should be a priority—to have clearly defined long-term goals as you move into the high school section of your travel basketball journey. If you know what your long-term goals are, it should guide your decision making throughout the process. For example, if your goal is to have your child adequately prepared to earn a college scholarship to a Division 1 program and to excel once they arrive, all of your decisions should come back to this goal.

The goal(s) that you and your family establish should be the constant reference for every decision. If your current program or team is helping you move closer to this goal, you probably want to continue working where you are. It doesn't matter who else is being recruited or who else is receiving McDonald's All-American votes. If your son or daughter is growing and moving toward his or her goals, then your situation is working well for you.

I have seen countless situations that were as close to perfect as you can get, but misinformed parents were focused on the attention other players on the team were receiving. They eventually moved their kid to another program because they thought their child should have been ranked higher nationally or receiving scholarship offers from programs in bigger conferences. The sad aspect of this scenario is that their kid was flourishing, and their recruiting base was widening. All the players I am referencing were on particularly good teams in established programs, but the parents' decision-making process was not based on a well-thought-out goal or plan for their child. A parent's decision to make a move can have a devastating impact on the child's recruiting and stunt his or her progress as a player.

I once had the opportunity to watch a rising team of elite ninth grade players who all played up. Their backcourt was SPECIAL! This backcourt was beginning to draw well over a hundred college coaches to their courts each game and all four guards played well together. It was entertaining to watch them play; as rising ninth graders, the offers were beginning to pour in for each one of the players. But one of the parents felt his kid should have been receiving more offers than one of the other guards in the four-guard rotation and, after causing dissension among the team, they made the move to another top national program.

I had the opportunity to see this player in one of the final showcases of the summer and it was disheartening to watch; he looked like a shadow of himself. The team was not as well coached and the pace they played at did not complement the player's skill set. The player did not receive as much playing time as he did on the previous team and he had very little impact in the game. The positive trajectory of this player from a development and recruiting standpoint was altered permanently and his college options were reduced immediately.

Although this player was completely happy with his former team and had long-term relationships with teammates, the parent's decision to make a change was based solely on what I call "Parental Pride." This can be avoided for so many players if families have defined goals that can guide them when outside influences provoke them to make quick (and oftentimes irrational) decisions. If your situation is benefiting your child, challenging them to grow, and helping them continue to expand their game, it is not important how many other players are receiving attention and what schools are recruiting them. As a matter of fact, playing with teammates who are being heavily recruited should be a positive for every player in the program! Playing for a program that has multiple players who are being recruited benefits the entire roster. It is important to embrace talent and competition because that is a microcosm of what the college basketball environment will be, once you arrive to your future college program. Once again, "iron sharpens iron."

5 PRACTICES TO AVOID MAKING DETRIMENTAL DECISIONS

1. DO NOT MAKE EMOTIONAL DECISIONS
Consider what is best for your child, long term. Remove yourself from the situation. Consider all factors related to your child and his or her growth and development as a person and player. Be sure you keep it exclusively about your child and not you as a parent.

2. SLEEP ON IT
Allow the emotion from a game, practice, tournament, or heated conversation to subside after a good night's sleep. This often allows everyone to have a more rational mindset and to see things for what they are, without the emotion. Parental pride can get the best of even the most rational parent, and this step can help parents avoid making decisions they may regret for many years to come. Keep it about what is best for your child, not about you.

3. TALK WITH YOUR SON OR DAUGHTER
What is bothering you may not be an issue for your child. Or, your child may not understand why you have issues with the dynamics of the team or program. Communication with your child is important, as the decision is going to ultimately impact them in multiple areas of their life.

4. TALK WITH THE PROGRAM DIRECTOR
Talk with the coach and program director before finalizing a move. You may realize that the program is the right fit for your son or daughter, but the coach or team may not be the right place within that program. You may also be able to work through what turns out to be a small problem after communicating with the staff. There will be times when both parties will realize that this is simply not the right fit for the player/family and the team/program. If this is the case, it is better to work through it properly, for many reasons. You do not want to destroy relationships because you failed to communicate properly. Travel basketball is a tight-knit community and college coaches will do their homework. It's important to communicate properly and, if you plan to leave a program, to do so with your relationship intact.

5. GO BACK TO YOUR LONG-TERM GOALS
Referring back to the long-term goals you and your family have established will help you remain focused and avoid decisions that could negatively derail your child's journey to success. Your long-term goals should always act as your rumble strips, warning you when you are getting close to running off the road.

Not the Right Fit

There are situations that may seem like the perfect fit. It appears that this is the team you have been looking for, and you have done all of the due diligence needed before making a decision to join a program. You do all the right things, have the tough conversations, meet future teammates, and go to workouts to experience the culture before you commit to the new program—and still things may not end up working out. This is part of life and why you must remain focused on your long-term goals.

My own son and daughter have both been a part of travel programs with different qualities. We experienced some where we liked everything about the program—they had a positive culture, strong infrastructure, and demanded player accountability, which we really appreciated. Then there were programs that, as soon as we started the journey, we knew were definitely not the right fit for us long term.

We were fortunate to make it through the entire travel season before we moved to a different program. Once we knew the program was not going to work for our family, we made every effort to make it through the season without leaving. I felt that as long as the environment was healthy and my son or daughter was still able to grow, we would make it work and take away the positive. I wanted my son and daughter to learn how to make it through challenging situations and grow while dealing with adversity. Looking back on those situations, they both grew as people and players, and those environments helped them to become more resilient.

Realizing that a team or program is simply not the right fit is part of the journey, but, again, I would also suggest that you keep those long-term goals close when finalizing your decisions. It is important to remember that leaving a program does not have to mean severing relationships. You never know what the future holds, and your son or daughter could end up rejoining that organization in the future, or that coach or program director could be the person a future college coach calls to get a reference on your child or your family. So, when making a decision to leave a program, do it professionally and do your best to leave on good terms.

Dysfunctional Environment

One man's function is another man's dysfunction. When you are a travel basketball parent, there is one thing you have to know before you begin this journey at any level: flexibility is not a suggestion; it is a requirement. If you are going to last the duration of the travel basketball marathon, flexibility will be a requirement for the entire family.

Sometimes you encounter situations that are beyond your control, such as changes to practice time and location at the last minute while you are driving, or receiving a text message saying you have a tournament on the upcoming weekend that is two days away and you already have family plans. These are real situations that many have experienced, and all are beyond your control and require you to be flexible. This is a part of what I call "the nature of the beast" of travel basketball.

However, you have to make a distinction between what is beyond your control and what is team or organizational dysfunction. Signs of organizational dysfunction often result in teams having to restart from scratch every year because parents have a difficult time dealing with recurring issues that a program should correct, but instead are the norm for that specific organization. These can be areas such as:

- Inconsistent and sporadic practices/going to tournaments unprepared
- Not receiving team uniforms/accessories after paying fees
- Inter-squad issues such as verbal/physical conflicts with players, parents, and coaches
- An overall negative environment that does not celebrate the team/program
- Coaches using substances or coming to practices/games under the influence

Each family has to decide which of their values are non-negotiable when and if they encounter a dysfunctional team environment. There are different levels of travel basketball dysfunction and each family will have to decide what they are willing to live with.

For example, I know some families that have made the decision that they do not want their son or daughter to play for a coach who uses profanity. In a situation like this, the family is holding to their value system and it is to be respected. However, this decision will reduce their options for potential elite level programs because, in the heat of battle, many coaches resort to using profanity, for a variety of reasons. This can happen at any level of athletics in any sport.

As you make decisions on what the non-negotiables are for you and your family, those decisions will determine the level of dysfunction you and your family will experience on this journey. The hope is that you are fortunate, you will not have to endure any negative experiences, and you can find a program that will help you reach your ultimate goal of playing at the college level.

#7

THE BLEACHERS

PARENTS, SOMEBODY IS ALWAYS WATCHING

THE BLEACHERS
PARENTS, SOMEBODY IS ALWAYS WATCHING

Parents, aunts, uncles, sisters, brothers, godparents... this chapter is for you.

If you have ever been to a travel basketball tournament, at some point you're going to experience the "bleachers." The bleachers can at times be equally if not more entertaining than the game itself. It could be two rival teams, a bad call by the officials, or a highly competitive game, but at some point the bleachers are bound to erupt.

I remember one occasion when, after entering a convention center for a showcase, I was standing at the top of the escalator. Looking down on the floor, I could see at least fifty courts filled with players and fans. Each court had games going and some courts had coaches packed on the baselines, scouting players. There were hundreds of fans watching as the teams battled intensely. I managed to squeeze into a tight spot in back of the college coaches as I tried to focus on a few players I specifically wanted to see. This was one of the few times I was able to watch a game without having to scout or coach. The game was turning out to be highly competitive and included Division 1 players of all levels on both teams, many of whom I had coached or trained in the past.

As the game started to get more physical, the bleachers began to get increasingly vocal, which is commonplace in travel basketball. Considering the amount of time most families commit to the life of travel basketball, the parents are often an extension of the player when it comes to game time. So, a little chatter is to be expected, especially when two rival teams are playing. However, in this game there were a few parents who began to openly and loudly criticize the coaches. The criticism continued to increase in frequency as well as escalate to demeaning comments. The comments became louder and louder and eventually one parent got up from his chair and began to walk to the sideline and yell out how he felt about the decisions the coach was making. By this time, the college coaches on the baseline were focusing their full attention on the parent who was going off about his child's travel coach in front of fans who were watching the game.

As I looked at the number of fans and parents watching what was turning out to be a great game between two elite teams, I could not help but think about the player whose parent was making a spectacle in front of the crowd and coaches. It's one thing to be loud and supportive from the bleachers, as many travel ball parents do, but this parent was humiliating the coach in front of hundreds of people—and, even more importantly, many of the college coaches from programs that had already extended offers to this parent's child.

As this parent continued to steal the show and berate the coach, I could hear the college coaches who were sitting in front of me share comments about what was happening. They spoke back and forth about how they could not deal with that as a staff. They realized the player had little control over what the parent was doing, but the coaches seemed to simply shake their heads as they watched this play out.

The following week, I was in the gym with the coaching staff of the travel team with the irate parent, and we discussed how they dealt with the incident. The head coach shared that immediately following the game, four of the local Division 1 programs withdrew their scholarship offers. Those coaches did not feel like their program could handle dealing with a local parent (who would likely regularly attend games over a four-year period), whose behavior was that disrespectful. They shared that having to deal with a family that could possibly disrupt their program's unity was not worth the risk.

This was a major decision for these head coaches, because this player was projected to be an impact freshman. The player

eventually signed with a program in a different region of the country. Although this player was an impact player, none of the local Division 1 programs made a scholarship offer, due to the parent's behavior observed in the bleachers.

"It is important to understand that coaches realize they are recruiting the entire family."

Even during non-live events, where college coaches are not allowed to attend games, someone is always recording and posting to social media platforms. Most event operators are also contracting to have games live streamed, as well, and the majority of the live-streamed games are available to be viewed months or years later. So, if you are a parent or relative of a player, it is imperative to remember someone is always watching. You never know who is sitting in the bleachers watching your child play.

Something else to consider is that Division 1 coaches will talk to travel and high school coaches about a player's parents and family to see if this kind of behavior is a common issue. College coaches have relationships on multiple levels; some even have relationships with gym custodians, and— trust me—when they are in the process of making decisions, they generally utilize all their resources before finalizing a scholarship offer.

As competitive as it is to earn an NCAA college scholarship, no player needs to have factors outside of the lines impact a coach's decision to NOT extend a scholarship offer when their heart is committed to a player. **While it may be challenging, it is necessary to do everything within your power to be positive during your child's game when sitting in the bleachers.** Controlling your emotions will help college coaches evaluate the player and appreciate his or her talent without an unnecessary distraction from the bleachers that could potentially shatter scholarship offers. Remember, someone is always watching.

#8

THE RIDE HOME

BIG PICTURE

THE RIDE HOME
BIG PICTURE

As he walked to the parking lot after watching his son play two games in a major showcase tournament, his mind was racing as he thought back through both games his son had played that day. *WE put in a lot of work on the court training over the past several months, specifically for this live period. He should've been more aggressive; he could've had more shot attempts. Defensively, he didn't press up on the ball—what's going on? We spent hours going over meticulous details for almost every situation: screen and roll reads, transition situations, separation moves to create space, hesitations, finishing at the rim, hours watching video on how to attack different zone defenses, as well as studying the mentality of the best pro players. On top of all of that, we even paid for a strength trainer twice per week. This is not what I envisioned; I'm heated!!!*

He couldn't wait to get to the car. *We have to talk about this, he thought. I even spent $40.00 for a weekend pass to watch the games.* He already had his words ready to start the one-sided conversation.

As they moved closer to the car, he noticed that everyone approached his son to congratulate him on playing a great game. "Good job out there today; you really controlled the game."

"Hey, that was an unbelievable pass at the end of regulation for the three!"

"Wow, that steal you made sealed the game for us."

"You really kept the team together today; loved your presence on the floor."

The father thought, *How could they say he played great today? He only had eight points in the game; college coaches want to see more than that...*

This is a common situation that has happened to many players and parents, and the example above is actually a true scenario. Yes, the father's last thought is amazingly accurate. College coaches do indeed want to see more than that—more than points, that is. All of the comments fans shared with his son while walking to the car are the exact intangibles college coaches come to summer games hoping to see.

So, this father's intention to let his son "Have It" in the car on the ride home was not a fitting response to the game had just finished playing. His son had actually displayed his complete skill set, which separated him from the other players that were on the recruiting board for his position. After playing a game where he had an opportunity to give a full display of his skills in a comprehensive way, every coach in the gym realized he was leaps and bounds ahead of the other players in this event. He showed he had the maturity to come in and play right away with the other talented players they had returning on their roster. After that showcase ended, and the weekend was over, his son received several more D-1 scholarship offers. Remember that these offers were a result of his son being put into an adverse situation, where he had to display his ability to control a game on both ends of the floor as well as lead his team in a highly competitive environment. This was a game most parents do not covet seeing, because it didn't include high-volume scoring.

Employ a Growth Mindset

Post-game conversations with your son or daughter can go a long way in motivating them to become even more effective as a player, especially as they develop the mental ability to grow from each game. Post-game conversations can also do the opposite for your son or daughter (if handled improperly); they can begin to create a multitude of issues that can chip away at their self-confidence. Going after them personally can also push them away from the game over time, as well as create issues within the relationship between you and your

son or daughter, creating tension that can extend for years after the ball stops bouncing.

It is important to realize that not even LeBron plays well every game, so we should all know that high school and middle school players will not play well every game, either. They are not going to play great every game and we should not want them to have their best game each time they compete (I'll address this specifically in later chapters). The goal is for your son or daughter to continue to grow as a player and person, and to be able to learn from situations and move on to the next play, the next game, the next practice, and the next day. This is called the "NEXT-PLAY MENTALITY." This is an attitude you can start to develop with your child and family from day one. It allows the entire family to have a growth mindset and to never get stuck in one moment that has already passed.

After all, even in life you go to sleep and wake up and live the next day!

Protect the Ride Home

The "ride home" is a special time and, if approached properly, can become a time that players look forward to because they get a chance to release the game with people who truly matter in their lives. Once they've had a chance to decompress, they can begin to look forward to the next opportunity to play and compete.

Just acknowledging the game will provide a great deal of confidence you will see immediately. It should build your child's mindset, so he or she becomes one of the most confident players in the world. This is a time during which many parents feel they should leave their child alone, but it could become a missed opportunity.

If your son or daughter has put in two weeks of preparation studying for a test in algebra, and if you've driven them to and from study sessions as well as helped them study for the test late at night, then on test day, when they get home from school, you fail to ask them about the test, what message does this send to your child? They may think you don't care or—just as bad—that it doesn't matter if they did well or not. So, after they have finished playing a game, to not talk to them, or give them an opportunity to at least share anything that is important, would be a departure from the constant commitment of supporting them.

I do want to be clear: it is not necessary to have a full-game review or go deep into analyzing their performance immediately after the game. But, it is important to acknowledge the game and invite your child's thoughts or feedback. It's a good practice to have more in-depth conversations later, not immediately after a game. There were only two areas that ever prompted me to address either of my children immediately after a game, and that was lack of effort and/or an attitude that was negative or indifferent.

PARENTS BEWARE! It's okay to talk to your kid after the game. Just be aware of bringing a negative reaction or attitude to the conversation. Don't get stuck on a bad play or a bad game. In reality, a bad play or a bad game is not always a negative.

"We all grow from setbacks and small failures. We have to keep the big picture in mind."

We can say something like, "Hey, it may not have been one of your best games, but we both know you've played better before and will play better in the future." If there are specifics that need to be seriously addressed, you can always discuss and then set a time to review video or get on the court to walk through the situation later. You want to provide a moment to discuss, but the remainder of the day or evening should not be spent processing the game. Allow them to have their moment, then keep it moving with their day. If you keep the big picture in mind and understand that this journey is a marathon and not a sprint, you will have an opportunity to transform your son or daughter's mental make-up and help develop the D-1 mindset.

So, the ride home should be a time that is not dreaded or feared by your son or daughter. It can become a time they actually anticipate, a moment to bond together and strengthen your relationship. This will help them realize that, whether a great performance or an average game, we process and move on because we are in this together. As a parent, it is important to remember that you have to be the one who remains consistent emotionally, understanding that one game does not define your child. It is your job to transform the ride home into an opportunity to create a bond that will last a lifetime.

As a parent, this is an area I wish I could do over again. I made major mistakes when it came to the ride home. I wish I had had some guidance in this area. I took every game personally. I often acted as if it were a direct reflection of me. I was unfair and just flat out a poor example of how a parent should have handled this area, especially one who played the game at the college level.

If there is one area of this book that you embrace, I urge you to detach and breathe after games. Give your emotions an opportunity to level out. The ride home cannot be an interrogation after every game. This could create barriers to your relationship that could be difficult to undo if the ride home always causes constant stress and tension. And remember, chances are they will be playing another game soon, so don't get stuck in that moment. Remember the Next-Play Mentality. The ride home can be used as a valuable tool to strengthen your child's resolve while also serving as an opportunity to teach him or her how to process and move forward.

PART 2: RECRUITING

#9

THE SEARCH

NARROW YOUR FOCUS

THE SEARCH
NARROW YOUR FOCUS

When you go to any live event, whether Adidas, Under Armor, Nike, or an Independent Showcase, the players and parents are all hoping college coaches will watch them play, like what they see, and be moved to learn more about them—and, at some point, extend a scholarship offer.

When you think about this rationale of hoping, wishing, and waiting for a college coach to notice you and your unique ability to help their program, it is contrary to every other process we go through when making important decisions. Generally, we investigate, research, and inspect the product, preschool, vehicle, or home we're considering before we decide or make a purchase. But, when it comes to recruiting, most families and players wait and hope that any coach will see them and like what they see and decide to extend a scholarship offer. This is a difficult way to play the game of recruiting, and many players and families have lost simply by not knowing the rules of engagement.

Regardless if you are a highly recruited player or have yet to receive an offer, this portion of your recruiting process is too important to leave to chance. I will give you a few important steps to follow that will help you increase your opportunity of landing an offer and eventually signing a letter of intent. But, before I share the first step in the process, you need to know there are two prerequisites.

PREREQUISITE #1
Evaluate Your Skill Set and Ability

To appropriately match the level at which you will be able to compete is important if you are going to have coaches take you seriously. One of the worst things you can do is misalign your talent and share that you want to play for a particular program that is not comparable to your level of talent.

One summer, I was taking my travel program to a different region of the country to compete in a showcase during a live recruiting event (college coaches would be in attendance). Before we left, one of the parents asked me if I was going to take the team to visit a particular university that was in the same city of the showcase because her child wanted to play for that university. Normally, I enjoy taking advantage of trips and creating time to do things like this. However, in this situation the mother thought her child would be able to play at this program, but this was a top-ten program nationally in one of the best conferences in the country. Her child was a good player, but this program typically signs players who are rated in the top fifty and McDonald All-Americans. My player was good, but was not a top 150 player and was also very undersized to play the position her skill set was suited for at a high-major conference. My player had the ability to compete at the mid-major level and potentially have a successful career at that level.

Being able to honestly assess your (or your child's) ability and pair it with the level of basketball you desire to play is critical in the recruiting process. In my estimation, the happiest players are the players who actually play.

PREREQUISITE #2
Know the Academic Requirements

Many universities have admission standards that exceed the NCAA requirements. Most families think that if you meet the minimum academic standards the NCAA lists on its website, you will automatically meet the admission standards of the schools you are interested in attending. I have known many students who met the NCAA standards but failed to meet the admission requirements of the institution they wanted to attend. A few of the athletes who did not meet the university standards had to attend a junior college for a year before being accepted by the school that recruited them.

Knowing the NCAA requirements for Division 1 eligibility is a must, and something you and your family should research once you enter high school. Being proactive and researching the academic requirements of programs of interest should be a priority. This will allow you to know what institutions have the best academic fit for you as a student athlete (or, if you are a parent reading this, for your child).

Now, back to how to successfully play the game of recruiting. You want to control the narrative. Regardless the level of your recruiting, controlling your situation is not only the most effective means to experiencing a successful recruiting process, but also the most efficient.

Step #1: Identify Programs that Fit Your Style of Play

This may seem simple, but many players receive offers and commit to programs that don't match their style of play, or they are blinded by the name of the university (as we say, the name on the front). Looking closely at style of play and the skill set coaches value will immediately narrow the programs and schools that should be attractive to you.

Coaches often recruit players whose skill sets do not fit their system but, due to an outstanding quality such as elite athleticism, an extremely high motor, or being a high-level defender, the coaching staff will try to work it out once the player joins their program. These risks can pay off for many coaches but, as a player, you should try to become as knowledgeable as possible about the program before you arrive.

Here is one principle to live by in the recruiting process: coaches may change locations, but styles generally remain the same. Watch the head coach's videos from previous years, even if he or she was at another program. Most head coaches learn a specific style of play and they tend to stay with that philosophy. Identifying style of play will help you to be aware of what you must learn or improve if you do choose to commit to a program that plays a different style or values a different skill set.

Step #2: Define Geographic Location/Climate in Which You Want to Live

Most players will spend four or more years in college, and many players continue to live in or near the locations where they attend college. Carefully considering where you want to live for the next four to five years (or longer) could be a variable that plays a major role in your personal happiness. Is having your family at your home games important to you? Many players want to enjoy their college experience with their family, so choosing a school within driving distance or a short flight away may be important for some players and families.

There are players who have a desire to go a specific school regardless of location or climate. I've talked to some players who wanted to play in a specific part of the country regardless of the distance from their homes. I can use myself as an example. I grew up in Phoenix, Arizona and, at that time, college basketball in the East dominated ESPN. I would watch all the games from the conferences in the East and I wanted to experience the cold weather and the East Coast lifestyle. This all factored into my decision to attend a university in the eastern part of the country. It was not a major concern that I would be over two thousand miles away from my family and friends. I can tell you, though, that it was challenging to come out of the locker room after a game and, for the first time in my life, not have a family member there to talk to.

Another factor that is important to consider is climate. If you live in a cold climate and the program you are considering is in a warm climate, will you able to make the adjustment? Most people would say that, naturally, that would be an easy adjustment, but it is still an adjustment you must consider.

Location and climate will be a factor in your everyday life as a college student, from the way you dress to how often you will see your family. These factors should be considered as you narrow your options. Carefully considering and discussing this with your family will allow you to make more confident decisions when the time comes to select your program.

STEP #3: Do the Universities Offer Your Major or Academic Interest?

When you are beginning to narrow your options of the basketball programs you are seriously considering, it is important to research the academic components, programs, and majors each university offers. There are only a few players every year who know they are one and done and will enter the draft lottery after attending school for one year. (On the girls/women's side, most players complete four years of university before they leave or enter the draft.) These players are less than one percent of the population of college basketball players. So, that means the majority of college basketball players will have to utilize their college degree as a professional in their field of study after graduation.

If you already know what you have an interest in studying in college, this will allow you to be more specific as you consider the schools to focus on in the recruiting process. And, if you are undecided on what you want to major in as you enter college, it is still a good practice to see what academic programs each school offers; you may find a few areas of interest as you learn more about the options each school presents.

Take Control of the Process

Following these steps will be a nonconventional approach to the traditional recruiting process many players and families have practiced in the past. It just doesn't sound rational that you should prepare all year, then suit up and travel to exposure events to wait and hope that a coach just happens to be watching a game you are playing in, then hope your performance happens to catch their attention. That truly is a recipe for stress and anxiety at a time when you are supposed to be at your best.

> *"The game of recruiting does not have to be a stressful and uncertain experience."*

Taking control of your recruiting will not only increase your chances of landing a scholarship, but it will also help you decrease much of the anxiety. This will give you a sense of ownership and direction that will connect you with coaches who will be a closer match for your skill set and talent level. Once you have followed the steps listed earlier, you will have a list of programs that fit your profile with style of play, location, and academics personally suited for you and your game.

The next step in taking control of this process is to contact the coaching staff of the programs that are on your list. If you and your family will be making direct contact with the coaches, I advise that you initiate the communication with a direct email to the coaching staff. I would direct the email to a specific coach, then copy the remaining assistants along with the head coach on the same email. Your initial email message should include personal information with these specifics:

- Name/ nickname/graduation year
- High school and travel program
- Position and strengths
- Significant awards and achievements that will distinguish you
- Brief highlight/mixtape (two-minute direction; see Chapter 11 for specifics)
- Direct message to staff: share why you have interest and what value you can add to the program
- Include schedule for current season; highlight most competitive games

After you have emailed the coaching staff, allow the coach between two and three days to view your information and hopefully discuss it with their staff as a group. Then follow up with a direct phone call to the coach you initially emailed. College coaches get bombarded with emails, text messages, and phone calls, so make sure you are prepared to communicate directly. Here are some key points to include:

- Introduce yourself

- Ask if coach has had the opportunity to view your video
- Share why you have an interest in attending and playing for their university
- Ask if they are recruiting your position for your graduation class
- Share your schedule and ask about attending their elite camp

These are key items that should be included in your initial conversation. Try to focus on incorporating the items listed above to accomplish your goal of finding out if they have an interest in you as a potential recruit.

If your high school or travel coach will be contacting coaches on your behalf, they should be familiar with the process and should be able to establish communication with the coaches and programs on your list. Following these steps will allow you to have a more focused approach to your recruiting while at the same time identifying programs that should represent many of the qualities you are looking for as you continue to further your basketball career and education.

I AM D-1

FACTORS IMPACTING COLLEGE DECISION MAKING

Family Should Guide
Principles of College Choice

College Choice Impacts
Your Future and Your Life

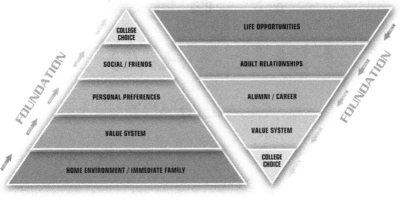

#10

ELITE CAMPS

COME READY

ELITE CAMPS
COME READY

The NCAA recruiting calendar makes it very difficult for college basketball coaches and players to truly build strong meaningful relationships. The calendar is filled with major restrictions on communication, including dead periods that prevent any communication and/or interaction between student athletes and coaches. So, college coaches try to, as they say, "kill two birds with one stone," and that one stone is their elite camp. This is the one opportunity that will allow you to play directly in front of college coaches, see the campus, work out with their staff, and compete against other top recruits. Elite camps are the one for sure opportunity where you will most likely see, meet, and work directly with the program's coaching staff.

Every year, I attend several elite camps during the months of June and August. At most of these camps there are scholarship offers extended during or at the end of the camp. If you want an exclusive opportunity to work out and play in front of the coaching staff you would like to play for in college, attending their elite camp is the best opportunity to grab their undivided attention.

Most colleges have one of their coaches work exclusively on sending out camp invitations to the rosters they get when they purchase tournament coaching packets. Every year in April and early May, they will normally mail the invitations. That is part of the business of college basketball and many of these camps could be helpful.

However, when college coaches want you to attend their elite camp, these invitations normally come by way of a call to your travel coaching staff or your high school coach. The invitations are normally done this way because they do not want to have a high number of players in this environment. They want to keep this environment as narrowly focused and highly competitive as possible. This is why you will not always see their elite camps advertised on their websites.

The NCAA requires every Division 1 program to post its elite camp for a certain number of hours, and they oftentimes remove the information immediately once they meet the time requirement. If you are not being recruited by the program whose elite camp you want to attend, you should contact someone from the coaching staff. Introduce yourself and let them know you have an interest in their program. Talk with them about why you want to attend their camp. If you are not comfortable doing this, you should ask either your travel coach or high school to contact them on your behalf.

"When you attend an elite camp, make sure you are prepared and in shape when you arrive."

Knowing that you will have the full attention of the coaching staff, be prepared to present the best version of yourself and to compete at the highest level. I have had the chance to see players elevate themselves and earn scholarship offers directly from performing well during elite camps. Every summer, I also witness players who were not on the radar with many coaching staffs before attending their elite camps, who, after having a successful camp, leave as a desirable target for the coaching staff.

Elite camps provide an opportunity for you to engage a coaching staff's undivided attention for an entire day. It will also provide them with an opportunity to see the intangibles they may not be able to pick up on when watching you play during a live period showcase game. Often, coaches want to know more about you as a person and have an opportunity to dialogue and get to know you. Coaches will also be able to see how well you are able to hear, see, and do.

Below are some features that are components of all elite camps, regardless of which school is hosting:

- University coaching staff
- Coaching staff runs and organizes drills and games
- Head coach is a part of the camp and evaluates players
- Features players the program is recruiting
- Recruiting decisions are made during camp

Being able to apply information quickly is important when you get to college. It will be important to compete on both sides of the ball. Getting "after it" defensively can and does catch the attention of any coaching staff.

When your opportunity arises to attend an elite camp, take it seriously, get prepared, and go ready to compete at your highest level. If you remember this saying, it will hold true for you: "The separation is in the preparation!"

Scholarship Offers

I hear and see them every day on Twitter and Instagram: player posts displaying all the offers they've received and the final schools they're considering. But what does it truly mean when you receive an offer?

If you receive an offer from a coach, what that means is that they see your talent and like you enough to make it publicly known that they want you to play for their university in the future. You will typically see the most advanced players receive college offers earlier than most. This happens for a few reasons; one is that they are simply among the best players in the country at an early age.

Another reason players may receive offers early is that they possess a specific skill set that a particular program values. For example, a player might be an exceptional three-point shooter. Spacing the floor is important and exceptional three-point shooters are rare, so if a college coach identifies a player who is able to shoot the three at a high percentage, he or she will probably receive more attention because that is a skill set that changes games.

I have also seen players who were special on-ball defenders, who could completely shut down elite offensive players. This is also a niche skill that can transform a college program. The players who are extremely exceptional in one area—enough that it changes games—may be the players who are also able to acquire college scholarship offers at an earlier stage. And, of course, there are some players who are simply better than most, and those players will receive offers from most of the top programs. These are generally the players who will also receive invitations to national events such as Team USA Tryouts and National Basketball Camps.

Rules of Engagement

While some players will have many options to choose, other players may only have one or even zero college offers. Some of the best players to ever play were not heavily recruited out of high school.

Even if you have only one college scholarship offer coming out of high school, you are still extremely blessed as a basketball player. That one offer is an acknowledgment of your hard work, dedication, and sacrifice being recognized by the leader of a university's basketball program. The fact is that many players never receive college offers.

Earlier I talked about the rules of engagement. Here are a couple to live by when entering the recruiting process:

1. Make sure you (or your child, if you are a parent reading this) is playing for a team where he or she can showcase his/her strengths. Winning is not the ultimate goal in showcase basketball, but rather competing and showcasing your talent.

2. Develop relationships early! Just playing and hoping a coach from the right school is watching is like throwing darts with your eyes closed. Be intentional and introduce yourself (or your child) to programs and coaches early. This summer, visit or participate in three to five elite camps. This will show coaches you are interested in their school and program and will help establish a relationship.

Following these steps can be a major help in playing the Recruiting Game. However, the most important thing you can do to help your scholarship opportunities is to make sure you are able to add value to a future college program. Constant mprovement, and making sure you can flat out play the game at a high level, will move coaches to be more receptive to your communication and reciprocate the interest. So, get to work on your game and maximize your potential to be sure the product is worth the advertising.

#11

MIXTAPES

THE BLUE PRINT

MIXTAPES
THE BLUE PRINT

Recruiting is the life blood of most college programs, and utilizing social media to share your talent is appreciated by college coaches. I recently had lunch with a head coach from a major program and I asked him what the top priority was for his assistant coaches; before I could finish my sentence, he answered ... "RECRUITING!!!"

In this section, we will explore the opportunities social media presents to bolster your efforts to market yourself and provide exposure to college coaches. If used properly, social media can be a platform as well as a conduit to help you contact college coaches and jumpstart your recruiting process. Unfortunately, when most people mention social media regarding high school and college athletes, they generally talk about the horror stories of athletes who made mistakes by posting inappropriate behavior. But, with some ingenuity and creativity, along with some technical know-how, social media can be an effective marketing tool for athletes seeking the notice of D-1 programs.

Social Media and Mixtapes

The recruiting game is officially global. It is challenging for college coaches to search the country—much less the world—to find every potential player with the skill set to catapult their programs to success. Most programs utilize scouting services to find players, not only in the U.S., but also internationally. Scouting services provide college coaches with names and breakdowns of players to review.

But even if certain players are not included in some scouting services, Instagram and Twitter provide a major opportunity for players to help promote themselves directly to the college coaches. An advantage that these platforms provide for players is that they both have the option of video uploads for coaches to watch.

I was eating dinner with my wife when a good friend—who is one of the top college coaches in the country—sent me a text message to ask if I knew a specific player who lived near me. I sent a message back and shared that I was familiar with this player. I told him I had seen the player at an exposure camp for the first time a few months earlier and that I was impressed.

I asked my guy how he had heard about the player. He shared that he had been scrolling on Instagram and had seen a brief clip of a player making an acrobatic finish at the rim and it caught his attention. He immediately did more research, and by the time he reached out to me he had already connected with the player's father.

Please take note that coaches do watch player posts and videos on both Instagram and Twitter. After watching a simple social media post, my friend started the recruiting process with this player and their family. The takeaway here is that your mixtape on social media can create opportunities and infuse your recruiting.

When constructing your own mixtape, it is important to include clips showing the following:

- You competing against top players/teams in your area
- All aspects of your game: on-ball defense, assists, rebounding, and leadership
- Your strengths on display: athleticism, shooting, energy

I AM D-1

ENERGY + EFFORT + ENTHUSUSIASM ➔ ENGAGED

PROPERTY OF I AM D-1 • PLAYER ENGAGEMENT • COPYRIGHT 2021

If your mixtape is comprised of a training session, be sure to include drills that show you making moves that mimic game situations as well working out with game intensity. Always provide a few different shooting drills. For example, if you're a guard, you may want to show clips of your training sessions with you shooting shots from a dribble handoff, being that many college offenses include dribble handoffs within the confines of their offense.

If you're a post player, you want to provide clips that display aspects of your footwork in the post, as well as your ability to step away from the basket to knock down threes. It is important to be intentional when you create your mixtape because it could be one of the only instances when a college coach takes one or two minutes to look at your game exclusively.

One final area many coaches have mentioned when discussing mixtapes is the music. College coaches have shared that it would be good for players to have music on their videos that does not need to be censored. Coaches often scroll through their social media while at home with their families or in social settings. Be sensitive to this reality and use music that will allow coaches to play or share your video in any environment.

Once you have completed your mixtape and are ready to post, be sure you tag the programs and coaches you are hoping will recruit you. As I stated earlier, college coaches do utilize Instagram and Twitter to scout and research players, and your video will more than likely be seen by more coaches than you may realize.

"So, remember to be intentional when putting together your mixtape; it just might be the key to initiating your recruiting process."

#12

D-1 MINDSET

TOTAL PACKAGE

D-1 MINDSET
TOTAL PACKAGE

mindset | noun
mìn(d)-set :
a mental attitude or inclination

I had been anticipating the match up with two of the top high school teams in the city. The gym was packed, and I ended up standing in a corner behind the cheerleaders. As I watched the game, one player's energy and effort jumped out at me. I noticed the passion and intensity; it was obvious this was more than just a game—the way he handled the ball, how he interacted with his teammates, and the intensity at which this player stared into the eyes of the coach during timeouts. I knew after watching him for two quarters that "ball was life" for this player.

I couldn't stop thinking about the way he played. After leaving the game, I was able to talk with his coach the following week. I had the opportunity to share what I observed after watching his player for a few minutes and the coach began to tell me what made this player special.

He said that after the dominant performance the previous Friday night, the player was back in the gym at 6:30 a.m. the next morning getting up shots on the shooting machine. The coach went on to say that this was indeed a mindset this player brought into his program as a rising ninth grader. He told me the player was also highly competitive, not only on the court but in the classroom, and that the player's competitive nature was different than most. It did not fuel him to focus on beating others; it was more an attitude that was intrinsically motivated. His competitive nature came from within: it was inter-competitive, and he was always working to be better than he had been the day before.

When I speak about the "*D-1 Mindset*," it is more than a level at which someone plays college sports. I'm often asked, "If it's not about the level of play for college sports, what is the D-1 Mindset?" The phrase "D-1" represents the highest level of performance. **The D-1 Mindset is a mental attitude that shapes your approach to everything you do in life. It is an attitude that supersedes your circumstances or situation. It is fueled by a desire to maximize your individual potential. This**

mindset produces a daily self-discipline that drives athletes to develop habits that extend past the norm. These habits go beyond the athletic arena and are often woven into all aspects of a person's life. This mental transformation results in athletes experiencing success in multiple areas of their lives.

The D-1 Mindset is made up of components that I call the "4 Cs." These components are interdependent of each other and they flow in this order.

1. COMPETE
2. CONSISTENCY
3. CONFIDENCE
4. COMPOSURE

Compete

The prerequisite for being a college athlete is the requirement to COMPETE. Competitiveness is what propels most athletes to reach their goals and arrive at the college level. College coaches do not coach effort, that is why COMPETE is listed as the first of the 4 Cs of the D-1 Mindset.

Players who compete at a high level are often driven to put in the most work. Training multiple hours per day, accompanied by school and homework, often refines qualities and distinguishes student athletes. As mentioned earlier, competition doesn't have to be external. Players who are internally driven achieve success independent of parents, trainers, and other outside supports. Possessing the desire to **COMPETE is an easily observable quality and, for those who possess the D-1 Mindset. this quality extends into other areas of their lives. It results in athletes handling their business on the court and in the classroom. Their drive to compete moves them to achieve success in whatever they touch. It shouldn't be difficult to identify those who have the first quality of the D-1 Mindset.**

Consistency

The second principle of the D-1 Mindset is equally important. CONSISTENCY is a must if embracing this attitude will become a way of life.

I often see athletes get hyped to play a specific team or certain player they want to prove themselves against. There's nothing like a little added motivation to amp up your competitive nature. But outside factors such as playing a team you've been waiting to get at, or a player you want to beat, is only temporary (situational) and doesn't last. Remember part of the definition of the D-1 Mindset involves "attitude," or way of life. **Consistency is the ability to sustain your level of competitiveness every time you are on the court, in the classroom, or working on other tasks you're committed to, regardless of the opponent or situation. Consistency keeps you from living from peak to valley.**

Think about the team that gets pumped up to play the team that won the championship the season before. They practice hard the week of the game and, when game time arrives, they play on emotion, compete at a high level, and may even win the game. But the next game, they play one of the worst teams on their schedule and come out flat and lose. This happens often and is an example of living from peak to valley. Performances are inconsistent and the level of competitiveness is not sustained. Athletes who COMPETE at a high level CONSISTENTLY establish a standard that separates them from their peers in multiple areas of their lives.

Confidence

CONFIDENCE is the third component of the D-1 Mindset. Athletes who COMPETE CONSISTENTLY tend to display and embody extremely high levels of CONFIDENCE. When you watch the most successful athletes at any level, they believe they can and will get the job done! Where does this CONFIDENCE germinate? How do kids at such an early age become so confident?

CONFIDENCE, as related to the D-1 Mindset, is a result of the first two components. The players who believe they can and will succeed regardless of the situation have subconsciously COMPETED CONSISTENTLY at a high level for years. **CONFIDENCE as related to the D-1 Mindset is the level of trust a player has in himself or herself to be successful in any and every situation. They do not entertain doubt!** This is not to be confused with arrogance; this self-reliance is a direct result of the hours spent COMPETING CONSISTENTLY at a high level over years. This level of trust cannot be manufactured; it becomes part of a player's muscle memory and mental DNA. This level of confidence is often exhibited in other areas of their lives.

Look at Steph Curry shoot a three-pointer and, while the ball is still in the air, he turns his back and starts to run down the court. Michael Jordan shoots a free throw but closes his eyes before he releases the ball. These are perfect examples of the CONFIDENCE that results from COMPETING CONSISTENTLY over time. CONFIDENCE cannot be purchased; it must be earned.

Composure

"Cool as ice."

"Ice water in the veins."

"Stone face."

It is 2017, the Women's National Semi-Final game. UConn has a three-year winning streak—one hundred and eleven games without a loss. It's the final seconds of the game and Morgan William, a five-foot-two (not a mistake, 5'2"!)

point guard gets the ball at the top of the key. There are four seconds left on the game clock in overtime. She dribbles to her right and, just before time runs out, she elevates over a defender and sinks a jumper as the buzzer sounds. The world is stunned, and Mississippi State does the unthinkable.

COMPOSURE is the fourth and final component of the D-1 Mindset's Four Cs: COMPETE, CONSISTENCY, CONFIDENCE, and COMPOSURE. While COMPOSURE may be the final piece to this puzzle, it is definitely not the least important. In relation to the D-1 Mindset, **COMPOSURE is the ability to be internally calm while simultaneously being able to operate externally with poise.**

4th Component of D-1 Mindset
COMPOSURE

The D-1 Mindset's definition of composure embodies more than being calm or poised externally. The internal calm is foundation to the external poise. I can recall athletes who appeared to be externally composed but internally their mind was unsettled, and their confidence was shaky. You may have witnessed players who seemed to be completely composed but when in a critical situation they may have shot an airball or made a mistake that is uncommon for them in a normal flow of a game.

I can remember being at a rec league game and the referee called a foul as time ran out. The player who was fouled went to the line with his team down by one, and the game clock was at zero. Before the official handed him the ball, he cleared everyone from the lane, leaving just the player and the rim. I glanced over at the bench and the coach was openly on edge, pacing back and forth.

Once the player received the ball, he went through what looked like a routine. He calmly bounced the ball twice, exhaled, lifted, and released the ball. While the ball was in the air, he held his follow through, and the ball went through the nets without touching the rim. The game was now tied, and his coach continued pacing the sideline. The official handed the ball to the player for the second shot and he followed the same routine as he did before. As he released the ball, he held his shooting hand up again with a fishhook at the top, the identical pose he'd made on the first shot, and the result was the same. His teammates rushed the court as the ball went through the net. This player was only in the sixth grade, yet displayed a remarkably mature level of composure during a pressure situation.

COMPOSURE is the bow that ties the D-1 Mindset together. During situations most people would view as nerve-wracking, players who put in the hours consistently possess the confidence in challenging moments that produces a sense of calm. The encouraging aspect of COMPOSURE is that, like the previous three components, it too can be acquired. As the saying goes, "The separation is in the preparation."

COMPETE + CONSISTENCY + CONFIDENCE + COMPOSURE = D-1 MINDSET

D-1 MINDSET
4 STAGES OF THE D-1 MINDSET

01
COMPETE
An internal drive to maximize your potential

02
CONSISTENCY
Competes every day, regardless of internal or external factors

03
CONFIDENCE
Strong belief in your ability as a result of hours/years of intense practice

04
COMPOSURE
Deep sense of internal calm, ability to operate under control in stressful environment due to excessive preparations

ALL STEPS ARE INTERCONNECTED.

PROPERTY OF I AM D-1 • D-1 MINDSET
COPYRIGHT 2021

I AM D-1.
ARE
YOU
?

DEDICATED

DETERMINED

DRIVEN

ABOUT THE AUTHORS

CHRIS MEADOWS

Chris Meadows, "Coach Chris," has spent over twenty years developing and mentoring some of the highest performing basketball players in the U.S. and several other countries. This includes developing and coaching over 1000 Division 1 basketball players and 12 McDonald's All-Americans, many of whom have continued to play professionally in the NBA and WNBA.

His work in travel basketball has distinguished him as a coach. He has won multiple national showcases on both the boys' and girls' travel circuits and served as the of Director of Player Development for several national organizations. Chris Meadows' imprint on the game of basketball has extended far beyond the court and into the lives of the players and families across the country. He has also worked exclusively with many college coaches to assist with player development during the summer months.

Chris earned a scholarship to play basketball at Saint Bonaventure University, where he completed his Bachelor's and Master's Degrees in Elementary and Special Education. He and his wife, Glinda, reside in the state of North Carolina. They have two grown children, a son and a daughter.

JEFFREY SHEARS

Jeffrey Shears is a joint appointed Professor in the Social Work Departments at North Carolina Agricultural & Technical State University and UNC Greensboro, where he is also the Director of the Joint Masters Social Work Program (JMSW). He earned his BSW and Masters in Education Administration from North Carolina A&T State University and his PhD in Social Work from the University of Denver.

Jeff's research interest is men (fathering, multicultural issues, HIV, and AIDS) and quantitative research with an emphasis on data sharing among social service agencies. He is co-author of the acclaimed *What All Dads Should Know* (2011). In addition, he has an extensive list of academic publications on fathering featured in national and internationally refereed journals. Jeff and his wife, Danielle, reside in North Carolina. They have 3 grown daughters.

I AM D-1 TAKEAWAYS...

NOTES:

I AM D-1 TAKEAWAYS...

NOTES:

I AM D-1 TAKEAWAYS...

NOTES:

I AM D-1 TAKEAWAYS...

NOTES:

ARE YOU D-1?

GET THE I AM D-1 MINDSET

If you are interested in bringing Coach Chris's empowering message to your parents, organization, and/or team, contact I AM D-1 Enterprises.

If you are a player and would like to work directly with Coach Chris in the I AM D-1 "MASTER CLASS Mental Training," contact I AM D-1 Enterprises:

Phone: (704) 649-7373
E-mail: mindset@iamd1thebook.com
Online: IAmd1TheBook.com
Twitter: @I_AMD1
Facebook: Facebook.com/@iamD1THEBOOK
Instagram: iamd1THEBOOK
YouTube: @I AM D-1

Sign up for I AM D-1's monthly e-newsletter at IAmD1TheBook.com

To purchase bulk copies of *I AM D-1: How to Conquer the World of Travel Basketball* at a discount for large groups, your organization/ program or team, **please contact our sales team at sales@iamd1thebook.com or 704-649-7373.**

9 781952 943072